DISCLAIMER

Supplies

PAINTS

Paints used are Delta Ceramcoat® Acrylics and Delta Ceramcoat® Gleams™. Please refer to individual projects for specific color lists.

BRUSHES

ROYAL® & LANGNICKEL
Bristle Series LW30 Flogger: 2"
Golden Taklon Series 150 Flat Shader: #4, #6, #8, #10, #12
Golden Taklon Series 250 Round: #2, #3
Golden Taklon Series 595 Liner: #10/0, #1
Golden Taklon Series 700 Glaze/Wash: 1"
Worn bristle round: #3 (for drybrushing)

BASIC SUPPLIES

Brown paper bag

Delta Ceramcoat® Gel Blending Medium
Delta Ceramcoat® Interior/Exterior Satin Varnish
Krylon® 1311 Matte Finish
Lint-free cotton cloths
Palette paper
Paper towels
Sandpaper, 400-grit
Saral Transfer Paper, blue and white
Sea sponge
Stylus
Tape (for securing traced patterns)
Tracing Paper
Water basin
Wood sealer

Please refer to individual projects for additional supplies.

Sources

In Latin America:
Laura Craft Studio
http://www.pinturadecorativa.com

Viking Woodcrafts, Inc.
1317 8th St. S.E.
Waseca, MN 56093   PH (800) 328-0116
http://www.vikingwoodcrafts.com

General Instructions

WOOD PREPARATION

Sand thoroughly with 400-grit sandpaper to achieve a smooth surface. Wipe off the sanding dust with a cotton cloth and then seal the surface with wood sealer. As needed to remove any raised grain, lightly sand the piece again, then wipe once more with a cloth to remove any dust.

BASECOATING

Use the glaze/wash brush to basecoat backgrounds. Apply two coats of paint, allowing the first coat to dry before applying the second. Once the second layer is dry, sand softly with a piece of brown paper bag. Wipe the surface with a soft cotton cloth to remove the dust.

TRANSFERRING THE PATTERN

Trace the pattern onto tracing paper. Center the traced pattern on the surface and affix it with tape. Put your transfer paper underneath the tracing (with the coated side down) and transfer the basic outlines with a stylus. Don't transfer the hairs.

PAINT CONSISTENCY

Use the acrylics straight from the bottle except for these special techniques:

LINEWORK: Add enough water to the paint so that it is an inky consistency.

MOTTLING: When using the Mottling technique, add sufficient water to the paint so that it is an inky consistency. There must be enough water so that the paint will drip from the brush to the surface.

WASH: Thin the paint with water so that there are two parts of water to each part of paint (2:1).

PAINTING LAYERS

Unless specifically stated in the instructions for a project or technique, let each layer of paint dry thoroughly before continuing.

FINISHING

Once you have finished your work, allow the paint to dry thoroughly. Apply two or three layers of Delta Ceramcoat Exterior/Interior Satin Varnish, allowing each layer to dry before applying the next. Sand lightly between the layers with a 400-grit sandpaper and wipe off the sanding dust.

Worksheet #1

Wide Awake Cat Eyes

Sleepy Cat Eyes

 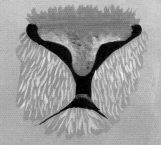 

Cat Muzzles

Zebra Nose and Mouth

mabel Blanco

Techniques

CRISSCROSS

Crisscrossing is used to create a background with multiple colors.

First, basecoat the surface with White, using a 1" glaze/wash brush. Allow to dry. Now, using a #12 flat brush (or other size to fit the area), apply three or more colors in sequence (side by side) on your surface. Since no retarder or blending medium is used, you must work quickly and in one small area at a time so that the paint does not dry. Next, use your flat brush in a random crisscross motion to work the colors together in all directions, achieving a smooth background with colors that are slightly blended together. Repeat the procedure until you have completely covered the surface. The final result should look like a blurry background.

DRYBRUSHING

Drybrushing is painting with a small amount of paint, using a dry brush. It is used to obtain a smooth, natural, transparent appearance.

Load a dry brush (I use a worn #3 round bristle brush) with a small amount of paint. Remove excess paint by wiping the brush on a paper towel, then apply smoothly over the surface using a circular motion.

FLOATING

The floating technique is often used to paint the highlights and the shadows on a project.

Dip your flat brush into water, then blot the excess water from the brush by lightly laying it on a paper towel, using no pressure. Load one corner of the brush with paint and stroke it on your palette to work the color across the brush almost to the other side. Then apply it on your project. The result must be a smooth transition of the color, fading towards the water.

MOTTLING

Mottling is a two-step process that uses the wicking action of water to spread paint in a random fashion.

First, basecoat the area using the color named in the instructions and let dry. Now, use a very wet brush to pick up the first color of thinned paint. Drip this paint color randomly over the surface. While the first dripped color is wet, repeat with a second color; you may also work with a third color. Each successive color will wick through the basecoat, spreading softly and providing a mottled effect.

PAINTING HAIR

When painting hairs, load the liner brush by rolling it in thinned paint, bringing the tip to a point. Blot excess paint by touching the tip to a paper towel.

Start painting hair using the following sequence: press, slide, and lift. By this, I mean that you should lightly press the brush down on the surface (not too much pressure; it is not a comma stroke). Pull the stroke, gradually releasing pressure on the brush, which allows the brush hairs to return to a point. Remember that for animals with short hair, such as the Panda, the hairs are always short, thin and irregular. Other animals, such as the Tiger, have longer hairs in areas, but these are also irregular in length. Always paint the hairs in the direction indicated by the arrows on the pattern.

The hair is applied in layers. The first layer is applied with the basecoat color of the animal + a lighter value. Each successive layer is lighter in value with the hair in the lightest layer painted with White. Using the drybrush technique, reinforce the light areas and the shadow areas using the colors stated in the instructions. Don't completely cover the previous layers. The longer hairs are done with a liner brush after you have finished applying the layers of short hairs. (See Worksheet #2.)

POUNCING

Pouncing adds texture, usually to a dry surface, using a different color.

Position the brush perpendicular to the surface and then tap the brush on the surface in an up and down motion. In this book, I pounce with a round brush, but pouncing can be done with any brush.

SOFTEN

To blur an application of paint so that it blends into the background, soften the edges of the wet paint by lightly brushing them with the tip of the brush. It should look slightly smudged.

WASH

A wash is a transparent layer of paint applied over a surface that has been dampened with water or a medium. It is used to achieve depth in your work. It is also used to enhance highlights, and to apply shadows and reflections.

First paint the basecoat and let it dry. Wet the surface with water or Gel Blending Medium. Load a flat brush with a small amount of thinned paint and apply it over the wet surface, blending the paint with the brush as necessary to achieve transparency. You should still be able to see the basecoat color underneath.

Little Tiger
Color Photos on Front Cover & Page 2

PALETTE
DELTA CERAMCOAT ACRYLICS
Antique White
Avocado
Black
Burnt Sienna
Burnt Umber
Cadet Grey
Chrome Green Light
Crocus Yellow
Dark Burnt Umber
Orange
Raw Sienna
Red Iron Oxide
White
Yellow

BRUSHES
Flat: #4, #6, #10
Glaze/Wash: 1"
Liner: #1
Round: #3
Worn bristle round: #3

SUPPLIES
Canvas, 16" x 20" (41 cm x 51 cm)
Krylon #1311 Matte Finish
Marine varnish
Unfinished oval frame, 19 1/2" x 23 1/2" (50 cm x 60 cm)

PREPARATION
No preparation is needed to paint on canvas. Transfer the design, allowing about 25 percent of the lower canvas area to be painted as the ground. Be sure to transfer all of the lines.

BACKGROUND
Using a glaze/wash brush, basecoat the upper background (not the ground area) with Avocado + Black (1: touch). Leave the area for the tigers the white color of the canvas. Now apply Avocado and Black using the Crisscross technique to provide a bit of texture to the background area.

The Mottling technique is used to paint the ground area. First, basecoat the ground with Burnt Umber and let dry. Now, use a wet round brush to randomly drip thinned Raw Sienna on the ground area. Drip a bit of thinned Dark Burnt Umber on the area that will appear under the mother's and baby's legs. These thinned paints will spread over the basecoat.

PAINTING INSTRUCTIONS
TIGERS
NOTE: When painting the eyes and muzzle, please refer to Worksheet #1.

Using the round brush, paint the Black stripes as indicated in the pattern. Remember that these lines must be irregular.

Basecoat the brown areas of the body of both animals with a mix of Raw Sienna + White + Orange + Black (1:1:1: touch).

(Continued on Page 8)

Little Tiger

Match and attach with the pattern
section on pages 8-9

8

Little Tiger
(Continued from Page 6)

Using Cadet Grey and the round brush, basecoat the chest, upper part of the baby tiger's leg, lower parts of the paws, the muzzle, over and under the eyes, and rims of the ears.

HAIR: Using the liner brush, start painting hairs on the brown areas with the basecoat color + White + Orange (1: touch: touch). Remember to thin the paint to an inky consistency. Overlap the edges of the Black stripes using soft, short brushstrokes.

Use Burnt Sienna to drybrush the contour of the baby tiger's head, inside his ears, over the nose, under the eyes, on the right side of the right leg, and on the paws. Use Burnt Umber to drybrush the shadow on the right side of the picture (up to the mother's leg), lightly on the right side of the baby's right leg, on the baby's body where it appears under the mother, and on the right side of the mother's body and leg. Drybrush under the mother's and baby's legs with Dark Burnt Umber.

Paint a few Burnt Umber hairs on the baby's paws and on the mother's left paw.

Continue to paint hairs on the brown areas, remembering that you must lighten the basecoat mix by adding more White and Orange (1: touch: touch) for each layer. Continue to paint lighter and lighter hairs in the lighter brown areas until the body is completely covered and you are satisfied with the result.

Paint White hairs on the areas that were basecoated with Cadet Grey, overlapping the brown areas. As necessary, paint additional layers until the areas are white. A few claws are visible on the mother's paws and on the baby's right paw. Using the liner brush with Black, paint a comma stroke to form the claw. Now paint a second, smaller, Cadet Grey comma stroke over the top of the black stroke.

EARS: Using the drybrush technique with the worn #3 bristle brush, reinforce the shadows with Burnt Umber. When dry, paint very short hairs using your liner brush and White that has been thinned to an inky consistency. Using the same brush, paint longer White hairs in the ear, extending from the outer rim towards the center.

EYES: Mix Yellow + Black + White (1: touch: touch) to obtain a green shade. Basecoat the iris with this color, using the #3 round brush. Also using the round brush, outline the contour of the eye with Black.

Add a touch of White to the green mix. Create a sparkle area by painting a comma stroke on the lower edge of the iris with your liner brush. Brush over it lightly with the tip of the same brush to soften. It should look like a transparent cloud. Once it has dried, paint the pupil with Black and let dry. Add a tiny dot of White to the sparkle area using the tip of the liner brush. Paint a tiny, broken White line on the inside of the lower eyelid and on the tear duct.

MUZZLE: Mix Red Iron Oxide + White (1: touch) and basecoat the nose using the #4 flat brush. Add a touch more White to the mix, then use the #8 flat brush to float highlights on the nose; soften using the round brush. With Red Iron Oxide, float the shadows on the lower portion of the nose in

Little Tiger

Match and attach with the pattern section on pages 6-7

the same way. Use the round brush to outline the contour of the nose and mouth with Black.

Paint hard, short White hairs on the chin. On each side of the muzzle, paint three lines of Black dots using the round brush. Using the liner brush, paint long White whiskers, starting from the two bottom dotted lines. With the liner brush and White, paint a comma stroke on the little tiger's mouth and then brush it with the tip of the brush to blur it slightly. Add a tiny dot of White just left of the center using the tip of the liner brush.

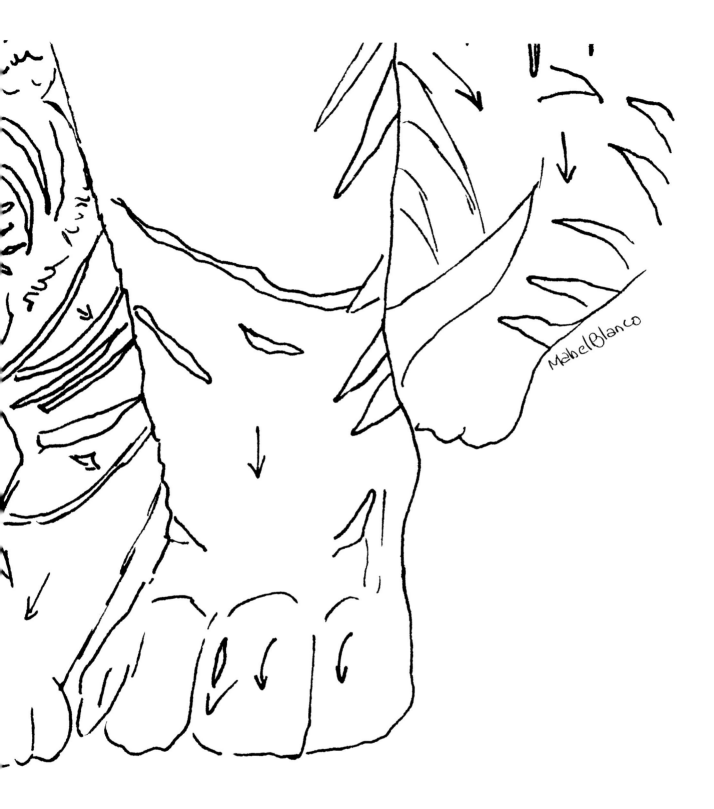

GRASS

Doubleload your round brush with Chrome Green and Crocus Yellow. With a loose hand, paint the grass, pulling the strokes upwards.

FINISHING

Using the glaze/wash brush, basecoat the frame with Antique White and let dry. Apply marine varnish and let dry for ten minutes. Using the same brush, paint the frame with thinned White. In a few minutes the varnish and paint will start to react, forming a rough surface. Allow twenty-four hours to dry.

Antique the frame by painting it with Burnt Umber and wiping the excess paint off of the frame with a cotton cloth. Let dry overnight and varnish with Krylon Matte Finish.

Black Panther

Color Photo on Page 11

PALETTE

DELTA CERAMCOAT ACRYLICS
AC Flesh
Antique White
Black
Bright Yellow
Burnt Umber
Colonial Blue
Orange
Raw Sienna
Red Iron Oxide
Walnut
White
DELTA CERAMCOAT GLEAMS
Metallic Pale Gold

BRUSHES

Flat: #4, #6, #8
Glaze/Wash: 1"
Liner: #10/0
Round: #3
Worn bristle round: #3

SUPPLIES

Film (plastic wrap)
Wooden plate with rim, 13" (32 cm) diameter

PREPARATION

To prepare the surface, please refer to the General Instructions at the beginning of this book.

Using the glaze/wash brush, basecoat the entire plate with two coats of White. Let dry, then transfer the complete pattern.

PAINTING INSTRUCTIONS

NOTE: When painting the eyes and muzzle, please refer to Worksheet #1.

RIM

Using the glaze/wash brush and Antique White, basecoat the rim of the plate and let dry. To create the texture, thin AC Flesh with water until it is a soupy consistency and paint the rim again. While wet, immediately press the plastic wrap on the surface (let it wrinkle a bit) and lift softly. Let dry and repeat the same procedure using a thinned mix of AC Flesh + White (1: touch).

(Continued on Page 12)

Black Panther

Black Panther
Pages 10 & 12

Mabel BlANCO

Black Panther
(Continued from Page 10)

WORKING IN THE INNER CIRCLE

Leaving the panther area white, use the Crisscross technique to create the background. Working quickly in small areas so that the paint remains wet for blending, start at the left side with Walnut. Apply the colors side by side, continuing to add more and more Orange to your brush as you move to the right; finish with just Orange in the brush. Blend the colors using the crisscross stroking action. Refer to the Techniques section at the beginning of the book, if necessary.

BODY

Using the #6 flat brush, basecoat the panther with two coats of Black, leaving the eyes white.

HAIR

The highlights on black animals are always painted in a light blue tone to give the impression of brightness. To create these highlights, use your #10/0 liner to paint hairs with a thinned, inky mix of Colonial Blue + White (1: touch). Paint hairs over the upper head, over the right ear, on top of the back, around the eyes, and on the right neck area immediately below the head. These hairs are short, thin and irregular. Refer to the pattern to note the direction of the hairs.

With Raw Sienna and your liner brush, add hairs on the outer contours of the face, over the eyes, and on the outer edges of the ears. Also pull some longer hairs out from the right ear. Using the worn bristle brush, drybrush Raw Sienna between the eyes in triangular shapes, decreasing towards the center and then bringing it up over the eyes.

EYES

Use the round brush to paint the eyes. Start by mixing Bright Yellow + Black (1: touch) to form a yellow-green color. Basecoat the iris and let dry. Add a bit of Black to the mix and thin it slightly with water until it is an inky consistency. Continuing to use the round brush, dab a bit of this color on the iris, wipe off your brush on your paper towel, and then pounce lightly to soften. Let dry and then outline the eye with Black.

Add a touch of White to the yellow-green mix, then paint a comma stroke on the lower edge of the iris and soften.

Now, paint the pupil with Black. To add a sparkle to the eye, use the tip of the brush to paint a tiny White line over the right edge of the pupil so that half of it is in the iris and half in the pupil. Soften the line (so that it looks transparent) and then paint a White dot over that line. To shape the tear ducts, use your liner brush to paint some thin, tiny White lines, following the shape of the triangular area.

Using the tip of your liner brush, paint a tiny White broken line on the black edge of the bottom eyelid. Use your #4 flat brush to lightly float Black shading across the top of the eyeball.

MUZZLE

Basecoat the nose using your #4 flat blush and a mix of Red Iron Oxide + White (4:1). When dry, add a touch of White to the mix and use the same brush to lightly float highlights around the nostrils. On the lower section of the nose, float shadows with Red Iron Oxide.

Use the round brush and Black to outline the nostrils and the mouth. Thin White and use the #4 flat brush to lightly float highlights inside the nostrils. Use the round brush with thinned White to paint a horizontal line to highlight the mouth. Using the liner brush, paint the short hairs around the nose and on the muzzle with Raw Sienna. Paint a few short hairs with Burnt Umber at the bottom of the muzzle and above the nose. Start painting the longer beard hairs with Burnt Umber, then switch to Raw Sienna, and then finish with White.

When the hairs are dry, use your liner brush to add four horizontal Black lines of tiny dots on each side of the muzzle, following its shape. Using your liner brush, brush mix White with a tiny touch of Raw Sienna, then paint long whiskers; they should appear hard and thick. Paint them loosely, starting at the muzzle and extending out.

FINISHING

Using Metallic Pale Gold, paint the outer and inner routed areas of the plate. When dry, apply two coats of varnish. Be sure to refer to the General Instructions at the beginning of the book.

Little Lion on Letter Holder

Color Photo on Page 14

PALETTE
DELTA CERAMCOAT ACRYLICS
Antique White
Avocado
Black
Burnt Sienna
Burnt Umber
Cadet Grey
Crocus Yellow
Raw Sienna
Red Iron Oxide
White
Yellow

DELTA CERAMCOAT GLEAMS
Metallic Pale Gold

BRUSHES
Flat: #4, #6
Glaze/Wash: 1"
Liner: #10/0
Round: #3
Worn bristle round: #3

SUPPLIES
Wooden letter holder, approx. 9 1/4" x 7" (23 cm x 17.5 cm)

PREPARATION

To prepare the surface, please refer to the General Instructions at the beginning of this book. Using Antique White and the glaze/wash brush, basecoat the entire holder and drawer, inside and out. When dry, transfer the complete design.

Create the background using the Crisscross technique with a #4 flat brush. (You may want to refer to the Crisscross technique at the beginning of this book.) Working in a small area at a time, quickly paint one color close to the other in the following sequence: Avocado, White and Yellow. While still wet, loosely blend the colors together using a crisscross motion. Continue to apply colors to the background, blending them loosely.

Let dry and then paint Metallic Pale Gold on the little drawer peg, on the edge of the base, and on the upper, routed edge.

PAINTING INSTRUCTIONS

Create a basecoat mix with Raw Sienna + Yellow + White + Black (1:1:1: touch). Basecoat the brown areas of the lions using your #4 flat brush. Basecoat the muzzle, chin, and over and under the eyes with Cadet Grey.

HAIR

Thin the basecoat mix to an inky consistency, adding a touch of White and a touch of Yellow. Using the liner brush, start painting the first layer of hairs on the brown areas. Add additional touches of White and Yellow for each successive layer of hair. As you paint each layer, pay attention to its growth direction as indicated in the pattern. Notice that the hairs are lighter on the rims of the ears. Paint White hairs in the areas that were basecoated with Cadet Grey, then let dry.

Drybrush Burnt Umber inside the ears, under the eyes, over the eyes (the eyebrow area), on the forehead, the sides of the nose, to separate the ears from the head, on the mother's body where the baby rests its chin, and all through the lower edge of the mother's body.

EARS

Reinforce the dark area inside the ears by drybrushing again with Burnt Umber. Mix Crocus Yellow + White (1:2), thinning it with water to an inky consistency. Use the liner brush to paint short hairs over the entire ear. Once these have dried, use the diluted mix to paint long hairs, starting on the inner-top edge of the ear and pulling towards the center.

EYES

The baby's eyes are almost closed. Paint the small portion of the iris that can be seen at the inner and outer corners of each eye using the round brush with a green mix of Yellow + Black + White (1: touch: touch). Paint the pupil Black. When dry, paint a tiny White dot between the pupil and the iris on the right side. Outline the eye with Burnt Umber.

MUZZLE

Using the #4 flat brush, basecoat the nose with a mix of Red Iron Oxide + White (1: touch). Add another touch of White to the mix and use this lightened mix to float highlights around the nostrils. On the lower part of the nose, float shadows with Red Iron Oxide. Outline the nostrils and paint the mouth with Black.

Drybrush the wrinkles that appear on right side of the muzzle with Burnt Sienna. Now use the liner brush and Burnt Sienna to paint tiny short hairs over the muzzle and just above the mouth.

In the muzzle area, paint four lines of Black dots on each side, using the tip of the liner brush. Whiskers extend from each of the dots on the bottom three lines. With a loose hand, paint thin, long White whiskers using the round brush.

FINISHING

When everything is thoroughly dry, apply two coats of varnish. Refer to the General Instructions at the beginning of this book for additional information.

Little Lion on Letter Holder

14

Leopard

Color Photo on Page 14

PALETTE
DELTA CERAMCOAT ACRYLICS
Black
Black Green
Burnt Sienna
Burnt Umber
Cadet Grey
Chrome Green Light
Crocus Yellow
Forest Green
Orange
Raw Sienna
Red Iron Oxide
White
DELTA CERAMCOAT GLEAMS
Metallic Pale Gold

BRUSHES
Flat: #4, #6, #8, #10, #12
Glaze/Wash: 1"
Liner: #10/0
Round: #3
Worn bristle round: #3

SUPPLIES
Sea sponge
Wooden tray, 20" x 15" (50 cm x 40 cm)

PREPARATION
Basecoat the entire tray with two coats of White, using the glaze/wash brush. On the upper rim, paint a coat of Red Iron Oxide; let dry. Dampen the sea sponge in water, then squeeze it thoroughly to remove as much water as possible. Now, using the dampened sea sponge, lightly sponge the rim with Metallic Pale Gold. Paint the inner and outer routed edges of the rim with Black Green. Inside the tray, transfer the ground line and the leopard pattern, being sure to transfer all of the spots as they help define its shape.

BACKGROUND
The green background behind the leopard is created using the Crisscross technique. You may want to refer to the Techniques section at the beginning of the book to learn how this is done. Use the #8 flat brush to randomly paint (in a crisscross motion) Forest Green, Crocus Yellow and Chrome Green Light. While still wet, blend the colors together slightly.

The ground area is done with the Mottling technique. To begin, basecoat the ground with Burnt Sienna and let it dry. Add water to Raw Sienna and pick it up with a wet round brush. Drip some of this color over the dry basecoat. While still wet, repeat the same procedure with Crocus Yellow and Chrome Green Light. Let dry.

PAINTING INSTRUCTIONS
LEOPARD
NOTE: When painting the eyes and muzzle, please refer to Worksheet #1.

Using a round brush, paint all spots with Black (including the back of the right ear). Remember that these spots are made up of hairs so they have irregular shapes.

Mix Raw Sienna + Orange + White + Black (1:1:1: touch). Use this mix to basecoat the rest of the leopard's body, avoiding the light areas of the chest, muzzle, around the eye, and on the right ear. Basecoat those areas with Cadet Grey.

HAIR: With the liner brush, paint the first layer of hairs on the brown areas with the basecoat mix + White + Crocus Yellow (1: touch: touch). Remember that the hairs must be short, thin and irregular. Closely watch the growth pattern of the hair as indicated on the pattern, overlapping hairs slightly on the edges of the spots.

Drybrush Burnt Umber on the forehead, under the eyes, behind the left ear, over the nose, behind the left leg (as you look at the leopard), on the leopard's back, between the toes on the paws, and under the jaw line to help define and separate the head from the neck. Also using the drybrush technique, reinforce the light areas on the feet and top of the right leg with White. Drybrush the shadows with Burnt Sienna, being careful not to completely cover the previous work.

The hair is painted in many layers. For each successive layer of hair on the brown areas, lighten the basecoat mix by adding additional touches of White and Crocus Yellow. Paint as many layers as you feel are necessary; don't be afraid to add layers to the drybrushed shadow areas.

Paint hairs with White in the lighter areas that were previously painted with Cadet Grey: on the chest, around the mouth and eyes, and on the white spot on the right ear.

Finally, using the #8 flat brush, float Black over the white hairs on the V-shape between the legs and under the face. Float Burnt Umber under the jaw line.

EARS: Using the worn #3 bristle brush, shade inside the ear by drybrushing with Burnt Sienna. Using the #10/0 liner, paint short, thin hairs on the rim of the ear with thinned White. Now paint long White hairs in both ears, loosely pulling the hairs in the left ear towards the center.

MUZZLE: Using the round brush, basecoat the nose with Red Iron Oxide. Add a touch of White to Red Iron Oxide and, with a clean round brush, stipple the highlights. Use a #8 flat brush to float a Red Iron Oxide shadow on the upper-right corner of the nose.

Using the liner brush, outline the mouth and paint the nostril with Black.

At the side of the muzzle (the whisker area), create horizontal lines by painting small Black dots with the liner brush. These lines should follow the shape of the muzzle and are short and irregular. Now with White, paint the whiskers out and slightly down, starting on the black dotted lines.

EYES: Use Crocus Yellow + White + Black (1:1: touch) and the round brush to paint the iris. Using your liner brush

(Continued on Page 16)

Leopard
(Continued from Page 15)

and Black, paint an outline around the iris and paint a small black dot at the twelve o'clock position to form the pupil. Now, add a touch of White to the iris mix and paint a comma stroke on the lower edge of the iris. Soften the edges and let dry. Add a touch of Black to the iris mix and use the #8 flat brush to float a shadow on the iris, under the eyelashes.

Using the liner brush, add a touch of White under the pupil and soften. Reinforce this sparkle by painting a dot of White, using the tip of your liner brush. Continue to use your liner brush and White to paint short eyelashes at the top and outer edges of the eye area.

GRASS

Doubleload your round brush with Chrome Green on one side and Crocus Yellow on the other side. With a loose hand, paint grass clumps here and there, pulling upwards from the ground and slightly over the bottom of the leopard.

FINISHING

Once completely dry, apply two coats of varnish. You may want to refer to the General Instructions at the beginning of the book.

Leopard

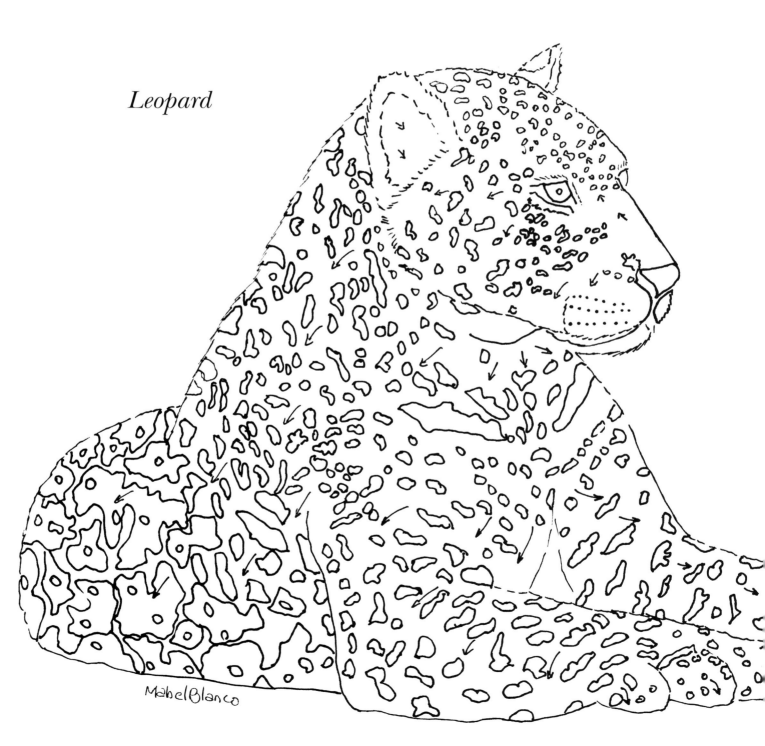

MabelBlanco

Lola
(The Small, Green-Eyed Kitten)
Color Photo on Page 19

PALETTE
DELTA CERAMCOAT ACRYLICS
Avocado
Black
Burnt Sienna
Cadet Grey
Raw Sienna
Red Iron Oxide
White
Yellow

BRUSHES
Flat: #4, #6, #8
Glaze/Wash: 1"
Liner: #10/0
Round: #3
Worn bristle round: #3

SUPPLIES
Krylon® Make It Last!® Clear Sealer
Krylon® Make It Stone!® Textured Paint, Travertine Tan
Wooden panel and oval frame, 13" x 11" (35 cm x 28 cm)
outer dimensions; 9" x 7 1/2" (24 cm x 19 cm) inner
dimensions

PREPARATION
Separate the frame and the panel. Refer to the General Instructions at the beginning of the book for information on preparing wood surfaces. Paint both pieces White using the glaze/wash brush and allow to dry.

Spray the Krylon textured paint on the frame and allow to dry. Apply the Krylon clear sealer to finish the frame.

Mark a division on the panel for two sections, allowing approximately 5" for the upper (sky) section and 2 1/2" for the lower (floor) section. Transfer the pattern.

UPPER SECTION
Using the #8 flat brush, place White, Raw Sienna and Avocado next to each other and lightly blend them using the Crisscross technique. Refer to the Techniques section at the beginning of the book if you need additional information.

LOWER SECTION
Refer to the Mottling technique in the Techniques section. Using the round brush, basecoat the floor with Burnt Sienna. Let dry. Add water to the round brush and pick up some

thinned Black, then drip this color randomly on the floor area. Repeat the same procedure with thinned Raw Sienna, allowing the water to react. Allow to dry.

PAINTING INSTRUCTIONS
NOTE: When painting the eyes and muzzle, refer to Worksheet #1.

Using the #6 flat brush, basecoat the entire cat with Raw Sienna + White + Black (2:1: touch), applying two coats if necessary. Using the same brush, basecoat all of the lighter areas with Cadet Grey. Using the worn bristle brush, define the paws by drybrushing with Burnt Sienna.

EARS
Using a worn bristle brush, drybrush the deep inside portion of the right ear, the lower-outer corner of the left ear, and in the inside rim of the right ear with Burnt Sienna. Using the liner brush, paint short, thin White hairs inside the ears. Using the same brush, paint the long White hairs, pulling the hairs from the bottom of the ear upwards toward the center.

HAIR
Using the liner brush, paint the first layer of hairs. Add a touch of both White and Yellow to the basecoat mix and then thin the paint by adding a touch of water. Paint the tan hairs, remembering that they must be short, thin and irregular. Follow the direction of the hairs as shown on the pattern. Paint White hairs in the areas basecoated with Cadet Grey.

Using the drybrush technique, highlight the light areas with White and create shadows with Burnt Sienna. Don't totally cover the hairs that you have previously painted. Continue painting layers of hair until you are satisfied with the result, adding a touch of both White and Yellow to the basecoat color for each successive layer of hairs on the tan areas. Paint short, tiny hairs on outer edges of the ears with thinned Burnt Sienna.

Paint White hairs to touch up the light areas (fronts of the legs, separating the hind leg from the side, muzzle, outer rims of the ears, top of the tail, and above and below the eyes). With the liner brush and Burnt Sienna, paint the hair that forms the stripes. Use short strokes for the hair on the body; the chest hairs are a bit longer.

Using the liner brush and Burnt Sienna, paint a thin comma stroke on each of the toes to form a claw.

EYES
Create a green eye color by mixing Yellow + Black + White (1: touch: touch). Using the round brush, paint the iris with this mix and then use the same brush to outline the eye with Black. Add a touch more White to the green mix and paint a comma stroke on the lower edge of the iris. Soften the edges and let dry.

Paint the pupil with Black. Then paint a White sparkle over the upper-left edge of the pupil and soften it. Thin the White

(Continued on Page 18)

Lola
(Continued from Page 17)

slightly and paint a thin line over the Black rim at the bottom of the eye and in the tear duct.

MUZZLE

Using the #4 flat brush, basecoat the nose with a mix Burnt Sienna + White (1: touch). Add a touch of White to the mix and lightly float the highlight areas in the center of the nose. On the lower part of the nose, float shadows with Burnt Sienna.

Using a liner brush, outline the contour of the nose and paint the mouth with Black. Using the round brush, paint some tiny hairs on the bottom lip with Black. Finally, float Cadet Grey on a small area under the line of the mouth.

Paint White tiny hairs on the chin and around the mouth; then, using the tip of the liner brush, paint three lines of Black dots on each side of the muzzle. When dry, paint the whiskers with thinned White. Do this with a loose hand, starting on the dots and stroking outwards.

After the entire cat has been painted, add some shadows to the ground below the cat using the Mottling technique with diluted Black.

FINISHING

When completely dry, varnish the panel with two coats. Assemble the panel and the frame. You may want to refer to the General Instructions at the beginning of the book.

Lola

Lola
Pages 17-18

Sparrows

Color Photo on Page 22

PALETTE
DELTA CERAMCOAT ACRYLICS
Antique White
Avocado
Black
Burnt Sienna
Burnt Umber
Cadet Grey
Colonial Blue
Opaque Yellow
Orange
Raw Sienna
Walnut
White
DELTA CERAMCOAT GLEAMS
Metallic Pale Gold

BRUSHES
Flat: #4, #6, #10
Glaze/Wash: 1"
Liner: #10/0

Round: #3
Worn bristle round: #3

SUPPLIES
Wooden octagonal remote control organizer box, 10 1/2" x 6 1/4" x 5" (26.5 cm x 16 cm x 12.8 cm)
Wooden paper pad holder, 5" x 6" x 1 3/8" (12.5 cm x 15.5 cm x 3.4 cm)

PREPARATION
Refer to General Instructions at the beginning of the book for information on preparing the wood pieces.

Basecoat both pieces with Antique White, using the glaze/wash brush and let dry. Paint the insides of both pieces and the bottom of the pad holder with Burnt Umber. Paint the edges with Metallic Pale Gold. Transfer the patterns.

PAINTING INSTRUCTIONS
BIRDS
NOTE: When painting the sparrows, refer to Worksheet #3.

Sparrows

Painting the birds is done entirely with a round brush, unless specifically noted in the instructions. For each bird, basecoat the head and back with Raw Sienna, the patch around the eye with Black, and the chest White. The brush strokes should be thin lines, soft and short, following the direction of the feather growth, as indicated on the pattern.

Paint the feathers on the back of the bird, using the liner brush and thinned Raw Sienna. Paint a second layer of feathers with thinned Burnt Sienna. Be sure the strokes follow the shape of the bird.

Using a mix of Walnut + Burnt Umber (1:1), paint short, individual lines to form the V-shaped feathers (wing bars) that appear on the bird's back. Paint a series of short, individual White lines between the dark V-shaped lines.

Paint shorter feathers on the head with Walnut, being sure to follow the shape of the head. Paint the feathers near the beak with a mix of Burnt Umber + Black (1: touch). Paint feathers over the white chest area with Raw Sienna. On the cheek area below the eyes, paint feathers with White; you may need several layers so that the feathers are bright white.

Under the beak, paint feathers with Black that has been thinned a bit so that when those feathers touch the white ones, they look grey. Outline the long tail feathers with Burnt Sienna. Let dry and then paint feathers with Burnt Umber, allowing some of the previous feathers to show through.

EYES AND LEGS: Paint the iris as a circle with Cadet Grey. Now, paint a smaller Black circle (pupil) within the grey circle. Finally, paint small White dots under the pupil, inside the iris. At the nine o'clock position on the pupil, paint a short White line and soften; when dry, paint a small White dot on the outer edge of the line. You may want to refer to Worksheet #3 for placement of these eye details.

Paint the legs with Burnt Sienna.

BEAKS: Basecoat the beak with Cadet Grey. Using the #4 flat brush, float a White highlight on the lower side of the beak. On the upper rim of the beak, apply a float of Black.

BOWL

Using the #10 flat brush, basecoat the bowl with Cadet Grey and let dry. Drybrush the shadows that appear on the lower-right and the inner-left sides with a mix of Cadet Grey + Black (1: touch). Use the same drybrush technique to add White highlights on the lower-left and upper-right sides of the bowl. Using the round brush, outline the edge of the bowl with White. Using the #10 flat, lightly float under the edge with Black.

To create the water inside the bowl, first paint a wash of Colonial Blue, using the #6 flat brush. Using the round brush, paint loose circular lines with Colonial Blue. Add wavy White circular lines between the blue lines. Float Cadet Grey + Black (1: touch) on the lower section of the water.

SEEDS

Using the round brush, basecoat the seeds with White and let dry. Paint Black lines on the seeds, making some lines thin and others thicker. Each seed is different. To give the seeds shape, float with Black on the rim of the each seed.

GRASS

Using the liner brush, paint grass blades with Avocado and Opaque Yellow. Use freehand strokes, pulling the strokes from the bottom of the blade upwards.

Finally, paint some simple flowers in the grass by making dots using the sharp end of a brush handle. Make four White dots to form the petals and a center dot with Orange or Opaque Yellow.

FINISHING

When the box is dry, apply two coats of varnish. Refer to the General Instructions at the beginning of the book, if necessary.

Tiger in the Water
Color Photo on Page 28

PALETTE
DELTA CERAMCOAT ACRYLICS
Black
Bright Yellow
Burnt Sienna
Burnt Umber
Cadet Grey
Chrome Green Light
Crocus Yellow
Magenta
Orange
Raw Sienna
Red Iron Oxide
Ultramarine Blue
White
Yellow

BRUSHES
Flat: #8, #12
Glaze/Wash: 1"
Liner: #1
Round: #3
Worn bristle round: #3

SUPPLIES
Canvas, 20" x 24" (51 cm x 61 cm)
Unfinished wood frame, 26 1/2" x 30 1/2" (67 cm x 77 cm)

PREPARATION
No preparation is needed to paint on canvas. Transfer the design. Be sure to transfer all stripes. Using the glaze/wash brush, start painting the background at the upper-left corner with a mix of Chrome Green Light + Black (1:1). As you move to the right, continue to add touches of Chrome Green

(Continued on Page 26)

Sparrows
Pages 20-21

Mabel Blanco

Worksheet #3

Sparrow

Eye

Seeds

Baby Bird Leg

Tiger in the Water

Instructions on Pages 21 & 26-27

Match and attach with the pattern section on
pages 26-27, then enlarge by 135%.

MabelBlanco

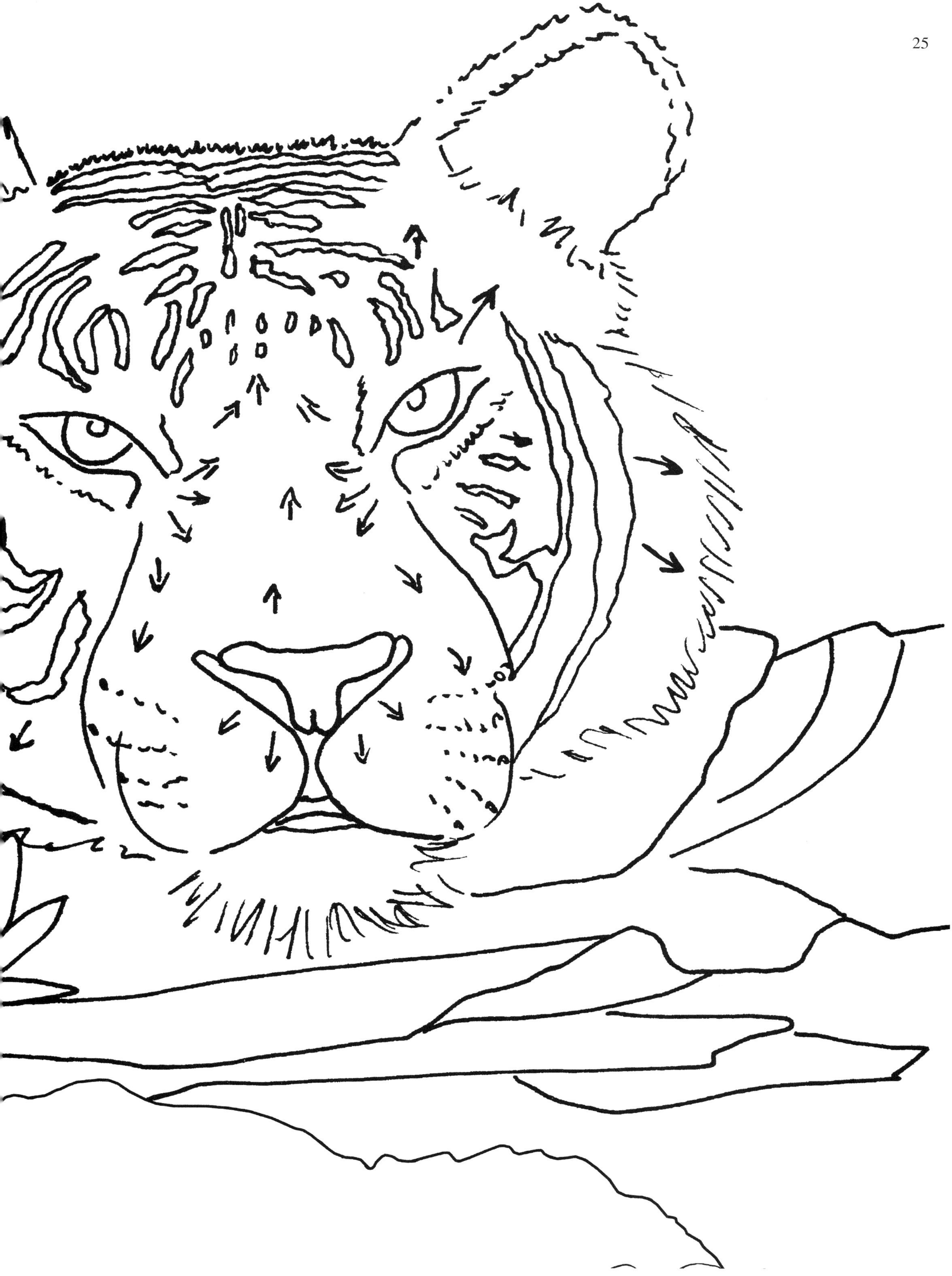

Mabel Blanco

Tiger in the Water

Tiger in the Water
(Continued from Page 21)

Light to the background mix to lighten it slightly. Leave the tiger and lily pads unpainted.

PAINTING INSTRUCTIONS
TIGER

NOTE: Refer to Worksheet #2 when painting the tiger face.

Using the round brush, paint the tiger's stripes with Black. These stripes are actually hairs so they must be irregular in shape to achieve a hairy appearance. Be sure your strokes follow the direction of the hairs as indicated on the pattern because these stripes give expression to the tiger.

Basecoat the brown/orange areas using a mix of Raw Sienna + Orange + White + Black (3:1:1: touch). (This will be referred to as the body basecoat color.) Basecoat the light areas with Cadet Grey. Basecoat inside the ears with Red Iron Oxide + White (1:1).

HAIR: To the body basecoat color, add a touch of White and a touch of Orange. Thin this mix slightly and use your liner brush to paint the hairs in the brown/orange areas, overlapping the black stripes slightly. In the light areas, paint the hairs with White. Using short, light brushstrokes, continue to paint additional layers of hair until you are satisfied with the appearance. On the brown/orange areas, add touches of White and Orange to the body basecoat color for each successive layer.

Using Burnt Sienna + Burnt Umber (1:1), drybrush shadows on the upper area of the muzzle and inside the bottom of the ears, being sure not to completely cover the previous strokes.

Using the thinned body basecoat color and your previous mixes for hairs, paint longer hairs at the sides of the head and on the chin. Some of these longer hairs are Crocus Yellow. In addition, add highlights by painting Crocus Yellow hairs on the face, circumference of the head, and on the left side of the body near the face.

EARS: Intensify the shadows in the center of the ear by drybrushing with Burnt Umber. With the liner brush and thinned White, paint short, transparent hairs directed towards the center.

The hairs on the rim of the ears are painted with the basecoat color. Add a touch of Crocus Yellow and a touch of White to the basecoat color for each successive layer, then continue to paint hairs until the rims are covered.

EYES: Paint the iris with a mix Yellow + White + Black (1:1: touch), forming a greenish tone. With the round brush, outline the contour of the eye with Black. Add a touch of White to the iris mix, then use the round brush to paint a comma stroke on the outer edge of the iris; soften this stroke to achieve a transparent effect and let dry. Paint the pupil with Black. Add a touch of White to Black and thin to an inky consistency. Dab this mix on the lower edge of the pupil, then soften. Using just the tip of the brush, add a dot of White in the center of the bottom edge of the pupil to reinforce the highlighting.

Paint some tiny White lines in the tear duct area and a broken White line along the bottom inner eyelid.

Using the #12 flat brush, float a Black shadow under the upper eyelid. Allowing the eyelashes to fall slightly over the eye, paint the eyelashes on the upper eyelid using your liner brush and thinned White. Also, paint a few eyelashes with thinned Black.

MUZZLE: Using the round brush, basecoat the nose with Red Iron Oxide + White (1:2). To this mix, add a touch of White and apply the highlights by stippling with the round brush. Using the #8 flat brush, float the shadows on the nose with Red Iron Oxide. Using the round brush, outline the nose,

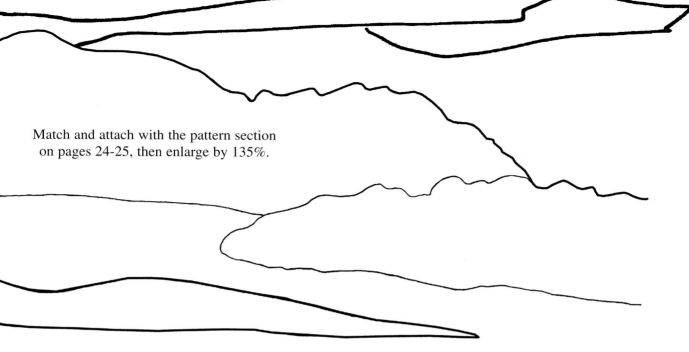

Match and attach with the pattern section
on pages 24-25, then enlarge by 135%.

and paint the nostrils and mouth with Black. Use the round brush and White to highlight the nostrils and mouth.

On each side the muzzle, use your liner brush to paint five lines of Black dots. Paint White whiskers starting from these lines. You may want to paint some Black whiskers immediately under the White ones to act as shadows.

LILY PADS

Using the #12 flat brush, basecoat the lily pad leaves with Chrome Green Light. Drybrush highlights with a mix of Bright Yellow + Chrome Green Light (1: touch). Since the light source is in the front of the tiger, these highlights will touch those areas that are closest to the viewer (you). The shadows should be applied on those leaves that are behind or under others, using a mix of Chrome Green Light + Black (1: touch).

Drybrush Red Iron Oxide + White (1:2) on the underside of some of the leaves. Drybrush Red Iron Oxide + Black (1:2) shadows on those areas where the leaves rest on the water.

Using the #12 flat brush, float Bright Yellow highlights here and there on the tops of the pads that are close to the tiger. Using the round brush, paint wavy Bright Yellow lines along the edges of some of the lily pads, dabbing a bit of paint here and there along the edges. (Refer to the color photo.) On those pads that are in the front, use the #12 flat brush to float White highlights. Use the round brush to stipple small, smudged White dots on the lily pads on the left that are close to the tiger's body.

FLOWER

Basecoat the petals with Magenta. Use the round brush and a mix of Magenta + White (1:1) to paint comma-stroke highlights in the centers and on the borders. Soften these strokes by brushing over them lightly with the same brush. Float shadows on the petals with a mix of Magenta + Ultramarine Blue (1: touch). The shadows appear on the petals that are behind other petals and in the V-shape between the calyx leaves.

The stem is basecoated, highlighted and shaded in the same way as the leaves. Using the #8 flat brush with White, float highlights on the right side.

The calyx is basecoated with Chrome Green Light. Using the worn bristle brush with Burnt Umber, drybrush shadows on the left side of the base of the calyx, following the rounded shape. Add a touch of White to your brush, then drybrush a highlight on the right side of the base, again following the rounded shape. Drybrush shading on the leafy parts of the calyx with Burnt Umber. Float highlights on the leafy parts with the #8 flat brush and Bright Yellow. Add a touch of White to the brush, then float again to reinforce some of the highlights.

WATER

To extend the brown and black stripes of the tiger below the water line, float thinned Black and thinned body basecoat color + a touch of Black, following the shape of the tiger. Float reflections on the water using a mix of Ultramarine Blue + White (1:2) and the #12 flat brush. Paint tiny White dots below the body of the tiger; these are reflections on the water. Below these dots paint another line of dots with White to reinforce these reflections. Using the #8 flat brush, float Ultramarine Blue + Black (1: touch) on some areas of the water. You may find it helpful to refer to the photograph.

FINISHING

To stain the unfinished frame, thin Raw Sienna with water to an inky consistency and evenly paint the frame using the glaze/wash brush.

Let dry thoroughly and then apply two layers of varnish to the frame, allowing each to dry thoroughly. Refer to the General Instructions at the beginning of this book.

Tiger in the Water
Pages 21, 24-27

Tiger
Worksheet #2

White Tiger
Color Photo on Page 32

PALETTE
DELTA CERAMCOAT ACRYLICS
Antique White
Black
Burnt Sienna
Burnt Umber
Cadet Grey
Chrome Green Light
Colonial Blue
Crocus Yellow
Raw Sienna
Red Iron Oxide
Walnut
White

BRUSHES
Flat: #6, #10
Flogger: 2"
Glaze/Wash: 1"
Liner: #10/0
Round: #3
Worn bristle round: #3

SUPPLIES
Wooden bed tray, 17 3/4" x 13 3/4" (45 cm x 35 cm)

PREPARATION
Refer to the General Instructions at the beginning of this book. Basecoat the design area of the tray with White. Transfer the design, except the paw prints.

Basecoat the contoured edges and the legs of the bed tray with Antique White, using the glaze/wash brush. Using the flogger brush, apply thinned Raw Sienna to these areas to imitate wood grain.

PAINTING INSTRUCTIONS
PAW PRINTS ON TRAY EDGE
Transfer the paw print design. Using the round brush, basecoat the prints with Cadet Grey and let dry. Pounce White all over the prints. Float White highlights and Black shadows using the #10 flat brush.

GREEN BACKGROUND
Paint this crisscrossed background in sections, working as quickly as possible so that the paint stays wet while you blend. Using your #10 flat brush, place Chrome Green Light, White, Black and Crocus Yellow next to each other, then blend them together with a crisscross motion of your brush. (You may find

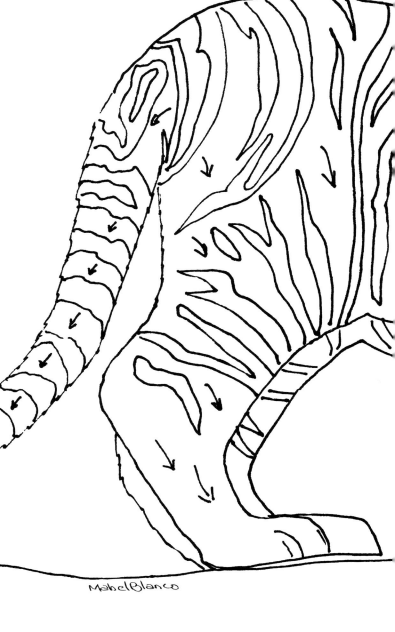

it helpful to refer to the Techniques section at the beginning of this book.) Repeat until you have completed the entire background.

ROCKS

The rocks are created using the Mottling technique as described in the Techniques section at the beginning of the book. Using a #10 flat brush, basecoat the rock area with Burnt Sienna and allow to dry. Now, pick up thinned Raw Sienna with a very wet round brush. Drip this color here and

there on the rocks. With this color still wet, add water to your brush again, then load with thinned Chrome Green Light and drip it here and there. With the previous colors still wet, once again fill the brush with water, load with thinned Black and drip it over several areas. Finally, drip thinned Crocus Yellow with a wet brush. Allow the water to freely spread the paint. Let dry.

(Continued on Page 33)

White Tiger

Mabel Bianco

White Tiger
Pages 30-31 & 33

White Tiger
(Continued from Page 31)

TIGER

Using the round brush, paint the tiger stripes with Burnt Sienna; these lines must be irregular so that they achieve a hairy appearance. Strictly follow the shape and direction of these stripes, as they give expression and shape to the animal.

Basecoat the rest of the tiger with Cadet Grey. Using the liner brush, paint the first layers of hair with White thinned with water to an inky consistency. Overlap the stripes slightly with these hairs, using short, light brush strokes. Continuing layering as necessary until the hair areas are White.

Using Burnt Umber, drybrush shadows under the belly, under the face, on the flanks, haunch, under the tail, down the center of the back leg, between the legs and paws, and on the exposed bottom of the feet, being careful not to completely cover the hair texture.

EARS: Mix Red Iron Oxide + White (1:1) and basecoat inside the ear with the #6 flat brush. Drybrush the inner part of the ear with Walnut.

Now, using the liner brush and White, paint short, transparent hairs inside the ear. On the outer rim of the ear, paint slightly longer White hairs. Paint the long hairs inside the ear with White. These hairs start from the inside corner and are pulled towards the center of the ear.

EYES: Mix Colonial Blue + White (1:1) and paint the iris using the round brush. Using the liner brush, outline the eye with Black. Add a touch of White to the iris mix and paint a comma stroke along the lower edge of the iris and soften. Paint the pupil with Black, then paint a White highlight on the pupil using the tip of the liner brush. Still using the liner brush, paint short White eyelashes. Add tiny White lines to the tear duct area, then use the #6 flat brush to float Black shading along the top of the eyeball.

MUZZLE: Mix Red Iron Oxide + White (1:1) and basecoat the nose using the round brush. Add a bit of White and float highlights above the nostrils. With Red Iron Oxide, float a shadow on the lower portion of the nose. Outline the nose and paint the mouth using the liner brush and Black.

On each side of the muzzle, use the tip of the liner brush to paint three lines of dots with Black and let dry. With thinned White, paint the whiskers, starting from the black dots and pulling outwards.

FINISHING

Refer to the General Instructions at the beginning of the book. Apply two coats of satin varnish.

Panda

Color Photo on Page 36

PALETTE

DELTA CERAMCOAT ACRYLICS
Black
Burnt Umber
Cadet Grey
Chrome Green Light
Colonial Blue
Raw Sienna
White
Yellow

BRUSHES

Flat: #4, #8, #10
Glaze/Wash: 1"
Liner: #1
Round: #3
Worn bristle round: #3

SUPPLIES

Wooden tray, 17 1/2" x 12 1/2" (45 cm x 32 cm)

PREPARATION

Using the glaze/wash brush, paint a wash of Raw Sienna to enhance the wood grain on the sides of the tray. (Refer to the Techniques section at the beginning of the book for more information on washes.) Using the glaze/wash brush, basecoat the design area of the tray with two coats of White. Let dry and transfer the design.

PAINTING INSTRUCTIONS

SKY

Paint the sky area around the panda, branches and leaves using the Crisscross technique with Colonial Blue and White, allowing some areas to be lighter while others are darker. (Refer to the Techniques section at the beginning of this book for help with the Crisscross technique.)

PANDA

Basecoat the head with Cadet Grey, using the #8 flat brush. Continue to use the #8 flat brush with Black to paint the areas around the eyes, the ears, and the lower portion of the body. Holding the chisel edge of the brush at a 45° angle to the surface, paint the edges of these areas with an irregular back and forth motion, forming furry irregular contours.

HAIR: Using the liner brush, paint short, thin hairs over the Cadet Grey areas with thinned White. As necessary, paint several layers of hairs to intensify the color. Be sure to pull the strokes into the black shoulder areas.

Drybrush Cadet Grey + Black (1: touch) to add shadows to folds of the head, next to the muzzle, above the eyes, and in a triangular shape over the nose. Paint a new layer of White hairs over these areas. Paint Cadet Grey hairs randomly (refer to the photo to see the placement of these hairs).

(Continued on Page 34)

Panda
(Continued from Page 33)

Using the liner brush and a mix of White + Colonial Blue (2:1), paint short, tiny hairs to highlight the black areas on the rims of the ears, around the eyes, and on the paws. Lightly drybrush Raw Sienna shadows on the head, neck, around the eyes, beside the muzzle, and above the nose.

EYES: Using the round brush, paint a circle with Cadet Grey inside the eye opening. Over the grey circle, paint the pupil as a smaller circle with Black, allowing the Cadet Grey to show a little around the edge as an iris. Using the round brush and White, highlight by painting a comma stroke on the upper-left edge of the iris and soften the edges. Paint two tiny dots of White on the upper-left side of the iris. On the lower edge of the iris, paint several tiny dots of White.

NOSE: Using the #4 flat brush, basecoat the nose with Black. With Cadet Grey, float a highlight on the upper rim of the nose.

BAMBOO BRANCHES

Doubleload your round brush with Raw Sienna on one side and White on the other, and then paint the branches, keeping the White side of the brush to the upper side of the branch. Highlight the branch by painting an irregular line of White on the upper edge. Outline the bottom edge with Burnt Umber. Float the separations between the segments of the bamboo with Black on one side of the separation and White on the opposite side.

LEAVES

Using the round brush, basecoat the leaves with Chrome Green Light. Mix White + Chrome Green Light + Yellow (3:1:1) and float lightly over some leaves. On other leaves, float a mix of Chrome Green Light + Black (4:1).

FINISHING

Apply two coats of varnish, allowing it to dry between coats. Refer to the General Instructions at the front of this book for additional information about finishing.

Panda

Panda
Pages 33-35

Mabel Blanco

Mabel Blanco

Zebras
Color Photo on Page 37

PALETTE
DELTA CERAMCOAT ACRYLICS
Black
Burnt Sienna
Cadet Grey
Crocus Yellow
Forest Green
Hippo Grey
Raw Sienna
White
DELTA CERAMCOAT GLEAMS
Metallic Pale Gold

BRUSHES
Flat: #4, #6, #8, #10
Glaze/Wash: 1"
Round: #3
Liner: #10/0
Worn bristle round: #3

SUPPLIES
Wooden octagonal box, 14 1/2" x 9 1/4" (37 cm x 25 cm)

PREPARATION
Refer to the General Instructions at the beginning of the book for information on preparing the box.

With the glaze/wash brush, basecoat the outside of the box with two coats of White. Basecoat the inside of the box with Forest Green. Transfer all of the design except for the details on the nose. Be sure to carefully transfer the shapes of the stripes.

BACKGROUND
The background for the box is painted using the Crisscross technique (leaving the zebras white). Refer to the Techniques section at the beginning of this book for specific instructions. Working quickly in one area at a time, use the #8 flat brush to apply Crocus Yellow, Forest Green and White in sequence, lightly blending them together with a soft, short crisscross motion of your brush. Continue the technique on the top and sides of the box.

PAINTING INSTRUCTIONS
ZEBRAS
Using the #4 flat brush, paint all of the Black stripes, remembering that these lines are hair so they must be irregular. Let dry and then paint the lighter stripes with Cadet Grey, being sure to follow the direction indicated on the pattern.

Drybrush the shadows with Hippo Grey to give shape to the heads and necks. Shadows appear under the muzzle, between the head and the neck, at the right side of the eye, along the bottom of the mane, and inside and under the ears.

The mane hair is stiff and has irregular ends. Painting the mane requires at least two layers of hair. The first layer of hair runs along the entire length of the edge of the neck and onto

(Continued on Page 40)

Zebras

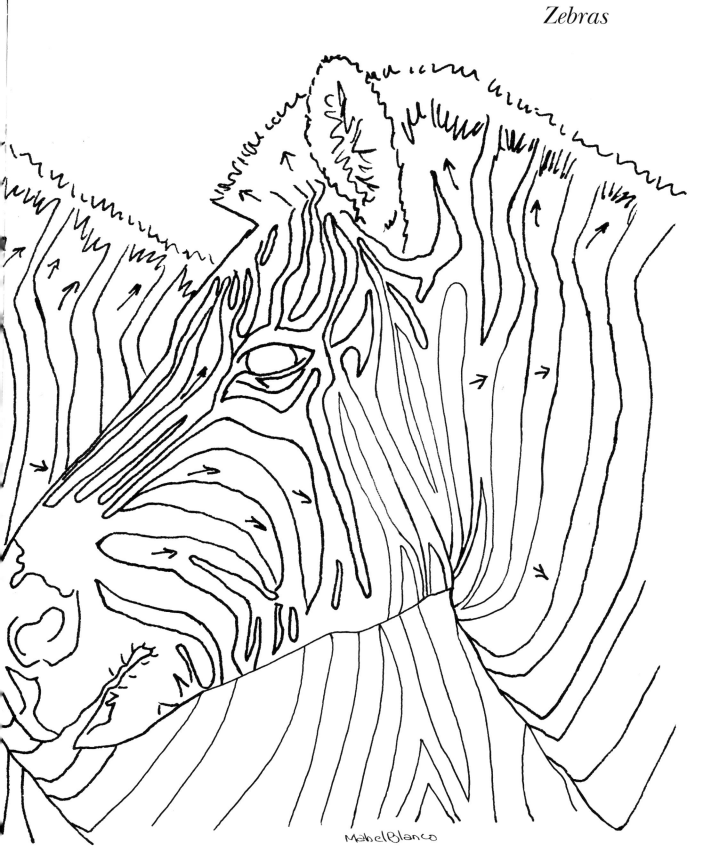

MabelBlanco

Zebras
(Continued from Page 38)

the forehead. Use your liner brush and Black to paint these hairs so that they appear short, stiff and jagged.

Use thinned White to paint longer white hairs at the ends of the white stripes, overlapping the first black layer slightly, without extending them to the edge of the black hairs. Paint a few longer, thin White hairs on the forehead of the left zebra.

EARS

Using the #6 flat brush, basecoat the inner ear with Cadet Grey. Paint the inner rim of the ear with a mix of Cadet Grey + Black (1: touch). Drybrush the center of the ear with Black.

Using the liner brush and thinned White, paint hairs from the rim of the ear to the center. Let dry. Paint plenty of them. Now paint short White hairs around the edge of the ear.

EYES

Using the round brush, basecoat the eye with Burnt Sienna. Allow plenty of time to dry. Paint a wash with Raw Sienna; imagine that you are painting a crystal ball, brilliant but transparent (brown inside and transparent outside). You may need to apply the wash several times, drying between each layer, to achieve this depth.

Using the round brush, paint a comma stroke on the lower edge with a mix of Burnt Sienna + White (1: touch). Soften. With the same brush, outline the eye with Black. Paint eyelashes with thinned White, and use White to paint a thin line on the inside of the upper eyelid and a thin, broken line on the inside of the bottom eyelid.

Very lightly, float White under the eye using the #6 flat brush. Finally, add a sparkle of White to the left side of the iris using just the tip of the round brush, along with a tiny White dot in the tear duct.

NOSE AND MOUTH

With the #4 flat brush, basecoat the nose and mouth with Hippo Grey, let dry and then transfer the pattern for the light areas. Now, paint the light areas with a wash of Cadet Grey and let dry. Mix Cadet Grey + White (1: touch). Using a very wet round brush, highlight the muzzle by dripping the mix over the nostrils, on the upper edge of the lips, and on the chin. While still wet, dip the brush in water, then drip a mix of Cadet Grey + Black (1: touch) inside and under the nostrils, on the lower lip, and on the lower curve of the left zebra's nose. Let the water react with the wet paint forming mottled shapes. *NOTE: You may find it useful to refer to Worksheet #1.*

Using the liner brush, paint the lines of the mouth with Black. Use the round brush to paint highlights with White around the nostrils, on the front of each muzzle, and in the center of the upper lip.

FINISHING

Using the round brush, paint the outer, routed rims of the box and lid with Metallic Pale Gold. When everything is dry, apply two coats of varnish. Refer to the General Instructions at the beginning of the book for more information.

Baby Birds

Color Photo on Back Cover

PALETTE
DELTA CERAMCOAT ACRYLICS
Antique White
Black
Bright Yellow
Burnt Sienna
Burnt Umber
Cadet Grey
Hunter Green
Orange
Raw Sienna
Territorial Beige
White
Williamsburg Blue

BRUSHES
Flat: #6, #8, #10
Glaze/Wash: 1"
Round: #2
Liner: #10/0

SUPPLIES
Film (plastic wrap)
Wooden box, approx. 8" x 5" x 2 3/4" (20.5 cm x 12.5 cm x 6.5 cm)

PREPARATION
Refer to the General Instructions for information on preparing wood surfaces.

Using the glaze/wash brush, basecoat the entire box with two coats of Territorial Beige. Let dry. Prepare a wash of Antique White + water (1:3) and apply over the surface of the box; while still wet, press plastic film onto the surface and lift off. You may find it easiest to work in small sections at a time.

Using the #6 flat brush, basecoat the borders of the lid and bottom of the box with Hunter Green. When everything is completely dry, transfer the pattern.

PAINTING INSTRUCTIONS
BABY BIRDS
Using the #6 flat brush, basecoat the head, wings, and the central line on the chest with Black. This should have an irregular border as you are painting feathers. With the same brush, basecoat the chest with Bright Yellow. Use Cadet Grey to basecoat the neck area and the light patch on the back of the bird at the right. (These are the areas that are white on the photograph.)

FEATHERS: Mix Bright Yellow + White (1:1). Using the liner brush, paint the chest feathers with this mix. These feathers are short, thin comma strokes that start on the upper portion of the chest. While moving down the chest, keep adding touches of Bright Yellow to the mix. The lower feathers on the chest are painted with thinned Burnt Sienna. Using the #10 flat brush, float Burnt Sienna over the area where the Burnt Sienna feathers were painted.

On the areas basecoated with Cadet Grey, paint White feathers using the same brush and procedure as used for the yellow feathers. Paint several layers, as needed, so that these areas look white.

Using your liner brush with a mix of White + Williamsburg Blue (2:1), paint small comma-stroke feathers to form highlights on the black areas. Apply these feathers under the head (the shoulder area where the wing starts) and on the head. These are the only feathers needed on the Black areas.

BEAKS: Since these are baby birds, beaks should appear slightly chubby. Using the round brush, paint the upper portion of the beak with Cadet Grey + White (1:1). The rest of the beak is basecoated with White. When dry, use the #10 flat brush to float Orange around the edge of this area. Form the split between the top and bottom beaks by painting an Orange line using the liner brush. Use the #10 flat brush to apply a float of Orange under this line. Continuing with the liner brush, outline the lower portion of the beak with Black.

EYES: Basecoat a circle on the eye area with Cadet Grey, using the round brush. When dry, paint a slightly smaller Black circle inside the first so that you can see only a small portion of the grey circle (the iris). With the liner brush, paint tiny dots of White on the lower edge of the iris. Paint a White comma stroke on the upper edge of the pupil.

BRANCH

With the #8 flat brush, basecoat the branch with Burnt Sienna and let dry. Using the same brush, float Black on the upper and lower contour of the branch. Using the round brush, form the veins of the wood by painting fine horizontal lines with Burnt Umber and Raw Sienna. When dry, highlight the center area of the branch with a very thin wash of White.

LEGS

Basecoat the legs with Black, using the round brush. To highlight the legs and toes, paint small parallel lines with Cadet Grey. You may find it helpful to refer to Worksheet #3.

FINISHING

Apply two coats of varnish allowing to dry between layers. You may find it helpful to refer to the General Instructions at the beginning of this book.

Baby Birds

Cat Book Box

Color Photo on Back Cover

PALETTE
DELTA CERAMCOAT ACRYLICS
Black
Bright Yellow
Cadet Grey
Chrome Green Light
Colonial Blue
Red Iron Oxide
Walnut
White
DELTA CERAMCOAT GLEAMS
Metallic Pale Gold

BRUSHES
Flat: #4, #6
Glaze/Wash: 1"
Liner: #10/0
Round: #3
Worn bristle round: #3

SUPPLIES
Delta Ceramcoat Brown Antiquing Gel
Old, scruffy flat brush
Wooden book box, approx. 6 7/8" x 8 1/4" x 2 7/8" (17.5 cm x 21 cm x 7.5 cm)

PREPARATION
To prepare the surface, please refer to the General Instructions at the beginning of this book. With the glaze/wash brush, basecoat the entire book with White. When dry, transfer the outer contour of the cat and the inner black areas.

The Crisscross technique (as described in the Techniques section at the beginning of the book) is used to provide visual texture to the background. Use this technique to paint the background around the cat with a mix of Chrome Green Light + Black (4:1) and Chrome Green Light, being sure to leave the cat area white.

PAINTING INSTRUCTIONS
CAT
NOTE: When painting the eyes and muzzle, please refer to Worksheet #1.

With the #6 flat brush, basecoat the light areas with Cadet Grey and the dark areas with Black, leaving the inner ears and the eyes white.

HAIR: Using a mix of Colonial Blue + White (2:1), paint tiny light hairs on the black areas on the top of the head, outer rims of the ears, and on the outer edge of the left black spot.

On the light areas that were basecoated with Cadet Grey, use the liner brush and White to paint short, thin, irregular hairs, following the direction of the hairs as shown on the pattern. Paint three layers of these hairs, completely covering the light areas, and allow to dry.

Using Cadet Grey + Black (1: touch), drybrush shadows between the eyes (over the nose). Paint a few short hairs with thinned White over the drybrushed area.

EARS: Drybrush the inner parts of the ears with a mix of White + Red Iron Oxide (3:1). Drybrush shadows in the ears using Cadet Grey + Black (1: touch).

Use your liner brush to paint short, thin White hairs at the edges of the ears. Loosely paint long, thin White hairs, starting from the bottom, inner corner of the ear and extending upwards to the center. Paint short, thin Black hairs at the inner-right edge of the left ear, on the left edge of the right ear, and extending slightly into the center of each ear from the head.

EYES: Mix Bright Yellow + Chrome Green Light (1: touch) and paint the iris using the round brush. Using the same brush and Black, outline the eye and paint the pupil. Add a touch of White to the green mix. Use the round brush to paint a comma stroke at the left side of the iris and soften. Using White, also paint a triangular-shaped smudge on the upper-right side of the pupil. Add a wash of Black (shadow) on the right side of the iris. Paint a soft sparkle of White with the liner brush on the middle-left side of the pupil. Finally, paint small, soft White lines on the inner tear duct area.

MUZZLE: Use the #4 flat brush to basecoat the nose with a mix of Red Iron Oxide + White (1:1). Add a touch of White to the mix and float highlights around the nostrils. On the lower portion of the nose, float a shadow with Red Iron Oxide. Using the liner brush, outline the contours of the nose and paint the nostrils with Black. Using the round brush, paint the mouth with Black.

Using White and your liner brush, paint long whiskers extending out from the muzzle. Now, using Cadet Grey, paint a few very thin whiskers under a few of the white ones. Add a few White eyebrow hairs, painting them upwards and out-wards. Also add a few short White hairs that just cover the lower edges of the eyes.

GRASS AND LEAVES
Using the round brush, load one side with Chrome Green Light and the other side with Bright Yellow. Blend the paint slightly on your palette and then paint some grass at the bottom of the box. Use loose brush strokes, pulling the strokes upwards. Between the green grass strokes, add a few grasses with Walnut.

Paint some longer, grassy branches extending from the upper-right corner of the box. Mix Chrome Green Light + Black (1: touch) and Bright Yellow + Chrome Green Light (1: touch). Paint these grasses the same way as you did the grass in front of the cat.

BOX
Using a glaze/wash brush, basecoat the inside and entire outside of the box (except the design area) with two coats of Red Iron Oxide. Let dry. On the edges of the box that represent book pages, paint with a heavy layer of Metallic Pale Gold.